Fishing

C O N T E N T S

Collins*Children'sBooks*

Gone Fishing!

So you want to go fishing? Well, you can head off for all kinds of angling haunts from a tiny pond to the open sea. You'll hook lots of different fish, big and small. And there'll always be the one that got away....

Canals and lakes

Canals are often neglected by anglers, so the fish they contain can grow big. There is very little water flow in a canal, except around locks. Lakes can be well-stocked with carp and tench.

Gravel pits

Many old industrial gravel pits have been flooded and stocked with fish. Carp, bream, tench and pike all grow to a good size in these deep waters. Heavy weed growth means there is plenty of food for the fish.

The river running by

From a slow-moving wide river to the smallest stream, rivers provide a haven for fish including some species which you will hardly ever find in still water.

In praise of ponds

Ponds are ideal places for fish to live. Your first tiddler might come from a pond. But don't be deceived, big fish can lurk in small ponds, and it's not unusual to catch a 4.5kg carp in a pond.

Estuary surprises

An estuary is the stretch of water where a river meets the sea. Estuaries can give an angler a surprise or two: sea fish such as plaice or flounder might be caught alongside freshwater fish.

CONFUSED?

There are three main kinds of fishing.
1 Coarse fishing: fishing for freshwater fish except trout and salmon species.
2 Fly fishing or game fishing: fishing for trout and salmon.
3 Sea fishing: fishing from a pier or a boat.

Hints for harbours

Harbours are great for fun fishing. The fishing is free, there are lots of different fish to catch, and you can take them home to eat! There's no need for fancy tackle either: some fish can be caught on a basic hand-held line.

EARLY WARNING

As an angler, you can be a watchdog for the environment where you fish. You will notice when things are not right. If certain plants or animals disappear, like this handsome kingfisher, it could be a warning sign that the habitat is in danger.

Tackle Tips

Going into a tackle shop can be a baffling experience! Here's your chance to find out what gear you need for a fishing trip and how it all works.

The right rod

Today's fishing rods are made from carbon fibre, or kevlar, or both. They are light, super-strong and measure from 1.8m to 4.5m. Hard-wearing rod rings are spaced evenly along the rod to hold the line in place.

You can handle it

The rod's handle, which holds the reel, is made of cork. It gives a firm grip, even when it's wet.

Handling carp

Carp rods have a two-part or 'abbreviated' handle made of a tough, spongy material called Duplon. The upper part holds the reel in position, while the lower part provides an excellent grip for a two-handed cast.

Get reel!

The fixed spool reel works to make casting the line easy. Once you start casting, the line comes off the spool in the same way as cotton from a bobbin. This reel makes it hard for a big fish to break the line.

With a centrepin reel the spool rotates as you wind in. The centrepin is favoured by river anglers and a similar reel is used for trout fishing.

Tempting grub

A swimfeeder is used to position groundbait close to the baited hook. A plastic tube is punched with holes and filled with bait and maggots which escape through the holes when the feeder is cast out into the water.

WAKEY WAKEY

If you fish at night, get yourself an electric bite alarm. Its bleeps and flashing lights will tell you when your bait has been bitten!

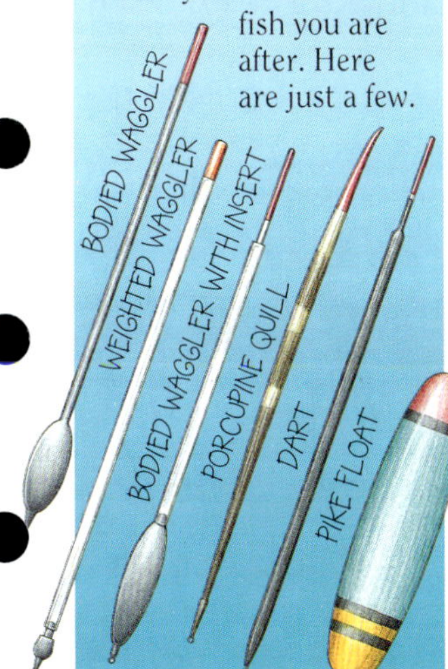

Floats

Floats do two jobs: their tops wobble to let you know when the bait has been bitten, and they come in a range of weights which support the bait at different levels in the water, so you can match your float to the fish you are after. Here are just a few.

Shot

Shot is used for float fishing. It ranges from tiny 'dust shot' to 'BB' size which weighs a few grammes. All shot is made from lead substitute, making it harmless to fish, birds and the environment.

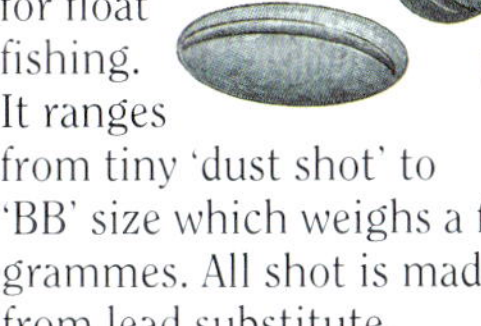

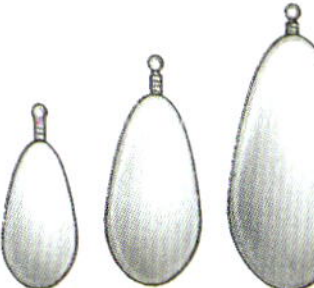

Heavy stuff

Lead-based legerweights, with a swivel at the top are used when fishing on the bottom. Ranging from 7g up to 225g (for sea use), they hold the line and baited hook close to the bottom and provide casting weight. (See page 11 to find out about legering.)

HOW MUCH?

Old fishing tackle is much in demand and some items fetch jaw-dropping prices. In 1988 a Richard Walker hand-made split-cane carp fishing rod was sold for £2,000 at a London auction.

More Tackle Tips

So you know about rods and reels, now read on to become a true pro!

Learning your lines
If anyone asks you what fishing line is made of, just tell them it's high tensile extruded plastic filament! The strength of the line or 'breaking strain' ranges from 14g (for hooking tiddlers) to over 90kg (for catching sharks). For most situations lines with a breaking strain of 1.5–4.5kg are used.

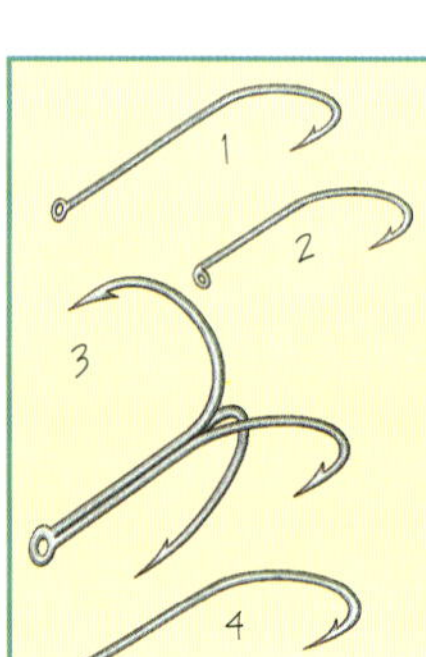

GETTING HOOKED

Modern technology has produced ultra-strong and incredibly sharp fine wire hooks. Hooks go from a size 1 (large) down to a size 22 (small).
1 Medium-shank straight eyed: use for carp, tench and bream.
2 Short-shank down eyed: general purpose.
3 Treble: good for pike.
4 Spade end: general purpose.

Net know-how
Landing nets are used to hoist the fish out of the water (it's impossible to lift big fish by line alone). Keep nets are bigger and you need one to hold your captured fish before weighing and releasing them. The biggest keep nets can hold a catch of many fish and are used in fishing competitions.

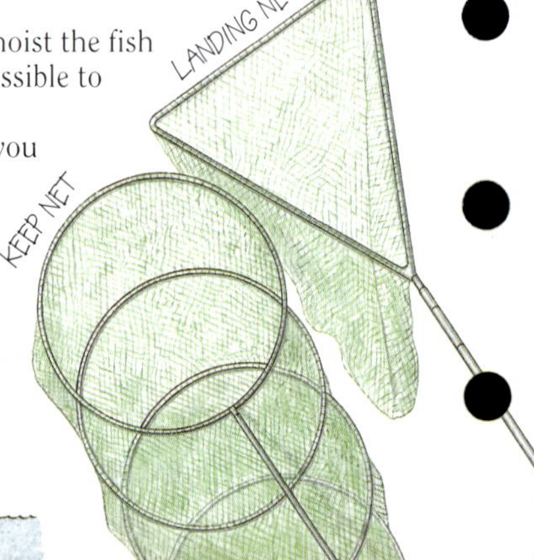

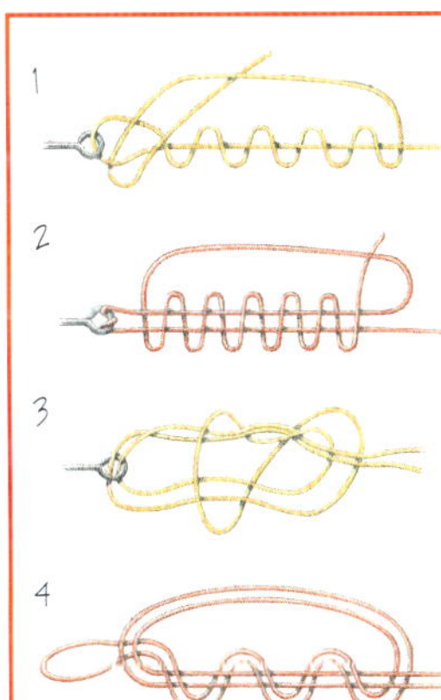

1
2
3
4

TYING THE KNOT

Knots are used for tying hooks, swivels, artificial baits and shorter lengths of wire or nylon to the line. They are also needed for anchoring the line to the reel. Follow these diagrams to get to grips with some of the more popular angling knots.
1 Half-blood knot.
2 Grinner knot.
3 Palomar knot.
4 Overhand knot (actually makes a loop in your line).

Creature comforts

A large umbrella will keep you dry and out of the wind. If you fish at night, a cosy bivvy is even better. Modern bivvies are big enough for a bedchair, a stove and your tackle. Warm waterproof clothing is a must when the weather is cold.

CARE OF YOUR CATCH

The ground where you fish will often be rough (and therefore unkind to fish) so it is vital that you use an unhooking mat. Bigger catches, such as carp, should be put in specially designed sacks. These keep the fish in semi-darkness, allowing them to recover properly after their battle!

Snap happy

The best way to record your catch is to take a photograph (it's illegal to kill coarse fish).

Fish Sense

If you want to catch a fish, you need to know what makes it tick. Each species has special features which you, the angler, should understand.

FISHY FACTS

Take a look at this fine perch for a crash course in fishy anatomy.

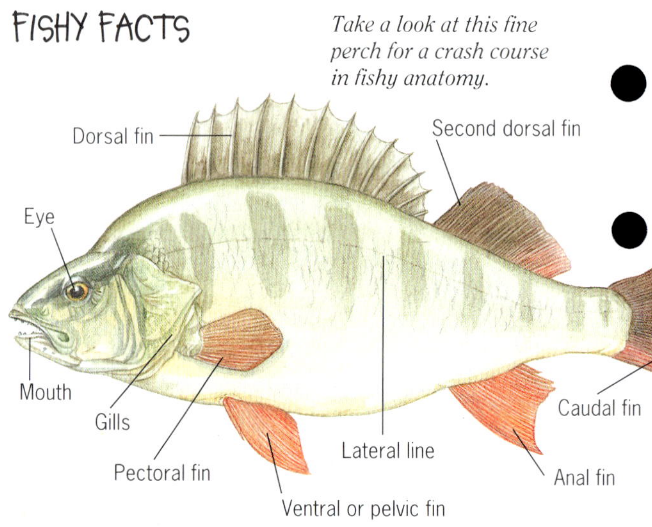

BREEDING BUMPS

Fish breed in the early summer. During the mating season male fish, like this bream, get little bumps called 'spawning tubercles' all over their heads.

So when you land a fish, you'll know how to tell whether you've caught a him or a her!

Tell-tale bubbles

When fish feed on the bed of a lake or river, they will give themselves away by releasing trapped gas. The resulting bubbles rise to the surface. Tench and bream produce tiny pinhead bubbles, whereas carp make huge bubbles. Mating fish thrash about in the water: that's a real giveaway!

ADAPTABLE MOUTHS

The mouths of fish are tailor-made for feeding. The carp is most at home in muddy ponds and its extendable top lip moves forward to suck up anything edible.
The barbel, which lives in fast-flowing rivers, is so-called because it has an underslung mouth with four large barbels or bristles on the upper lip. These sensitive barbels can find food on the river bed.

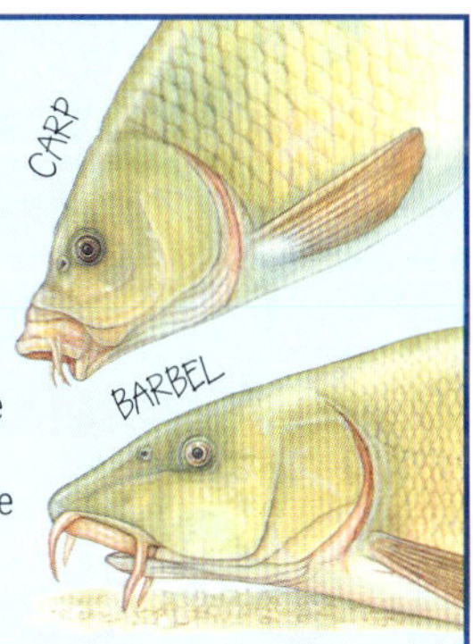

A SIZE GUIDE

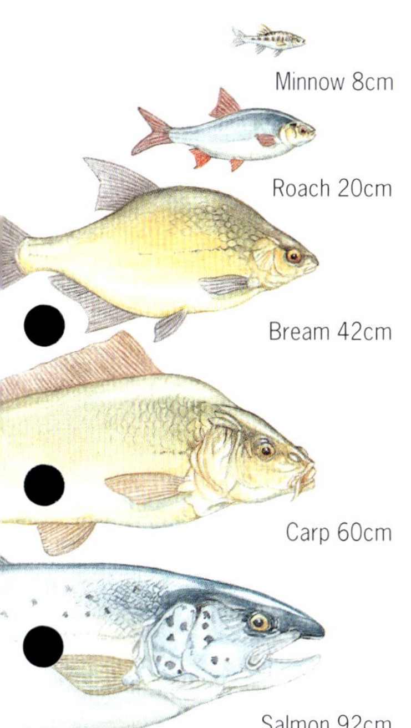

Minnow 8cm

Roach 20cm

Bream 42cm

Carp 60cm

Salmon 92cm

THE ANGLER'S CODE

1 Never start to fish without first obtaining a rod licence – these are available from all Post Offices.
2 Although there is some free fishing, most waters where you are allowed to fish are controlled by angling clubs.
3 Visit your local tackle shop to find out where you can fish.
4 Keep to the Countryside Code and club rules.
5 Look after the fish you catch, return all coarse fish to the water as soon as possible.

Classic Catches

The fish anglers most want to catch is a carp. Growing to over 10kg, carp are tough fighters and keen anglers are always after the elusive 'big one'. Tench and bream follow closely in the popularity stakes.

COMMON CARP

MIRROR CARP

KNOW YOUR CARP

The common carp has large golden scales all over its body.

LEATHER CARP

The rare leather carp has no scales: its skin looks and feels like leather!

The mirror carp gets its name from the shimmering scales scattered over its body.

Crucian carp are small, stumpy fish! Unlike most other carp, they have no barbels.

CRUCIAN CARP

OAP!

Carp are said to be the longest-living coarse fish. Some fish are on record as being nearly 70 years old. All the more reason to look after your catch.

Where and when?
You'll find carp in almost any piece of water. Purists catch carp in the hours of darkness, but you can be lucky at any time of day or night.

Your bait box
Boilies – specially made balls of bait – are perfect for carp. They come in loads of flavours and colours.

LEGERING

Carp, tench and bream all feed on the river bed. Legering lets you outwit these fish. Fixing your bait up with a legerweight makes the bait and hook sink quickly to the bottom. The simplest way to present your bait is to fix a legerweight on the line, stopped by a swivel. A short length of line (or trace) is tied to this swivel. The trace has the hook at its other end.

Tale of the tench

Lovely red eyes and a freshly-lacquered appearance make the tench a handsome fish. It often grows to about 2.5kg in weight. Its favourite haunt is among lily beds, so this is where tench anglers will fish, waiting for the tell-tale feeding bubbles.

Brush up on bream

Bream up to 600g are known as skimmers. When they grow bigger it's trickier tempting them onto the hook. The biggest weigh in at 6kg and are only caught by real bream fanatics!

DID YOU KNOW?

Goldfish are a kind of carp. If they get too big for their bowl, people sometimes dump them into a local river where they can grow to a mammoth 5kg. Phew!

Life in the Fast Lane

If you want to catch barbel, chub, gudgeon or dace, head for the fastest-flowing stretches of the river.

REACH FOR YOUR SWIMFEEDER

This gadget holds a good supply of groundbait close to the hook. When full, the heavy swimfeeder also acts as a legerweight. Holes in the feeder allow the bait to be flushed out.

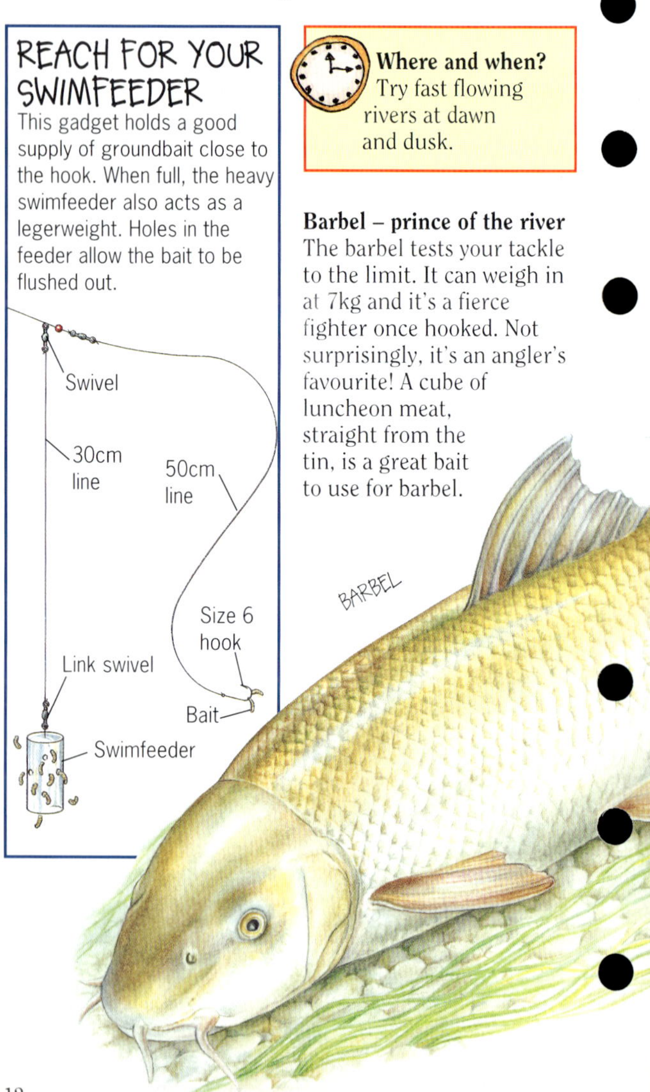

Where and when? Try fast flowing rivers at dawn and dusk.

Barbel – prince of the river
The barbel tests your tackle to the limit. It can weigh in at 7kg and it's a fierce fighter once hooked. Not surprisingly, it's an angler's favourite! A cube of luncheon meat, straight from the tin, is a great bait to use for barbel.

Bait box extra!
Chub are rather partial to freshwater crayfish (which look like little lobsters). Mount them whole on a size 2 hook.

CHUB

Ol' rubber lips
The chub is a powerful fish with a huge mouth. It will scoff all kinds of bait including bread crust, dead fish, offal, slugs and even the leftovers of your Sunday lunch!

GUDGEON

Small fry
Gudgeon is one of the smaller fish you will catch in a river. As most rivers are infested with them, you will find they are constantly after your bait. This can make life difficult when you want to catch something else.

DACE

Dainty dace
Sometimes called the 'silver lady' of the stream, the dace rarely grows over 500g, but it will still put up a fight. Maggots are the best bait for dace.

FRYING TONIGHT
In Victorian times, the English gentry held summer gudgeon parties on the River Thames. These lavish affairs ended with the catch being cooked for a picnic. Fried gudgeon is still a delicacy in France.

Roach and Co.

From trotting to trapping, it's amazing what lengths anglers will go to for that prize catch!

The roving roach

The roach is one of the most widespread freshwater fish species in Europe. It has a taste for even the most exotic baits, but any piece of bread or a humble maggot will tempt this colourful fish.

Red rudd

A close relative of the roach, the rudd is more brightly coloured. It has distinctive blood red fins and a protruding upper lip. Unlike the roach, it will happily feed near the surface, sipping down dead flies or, if it's unlucky, an angler's bait!

When?
Roach and rudd feed day and night. However, the most experienced anglers will try for them either in the heat of they day, or just before dusk.

Your bait box
Best baits for roach and rudd are bread, sweetcorn, maggots, casters (dead maggots), worms and – believe it or not – a fly!

14

TROTTING

You'll get most success from this method if you use a centrepin reel. The float 'trots' downstream with the flow of the river which in turn is strong enough to pull line slowly off the reel. The trick is to match the reel's speed to the flow of the water.

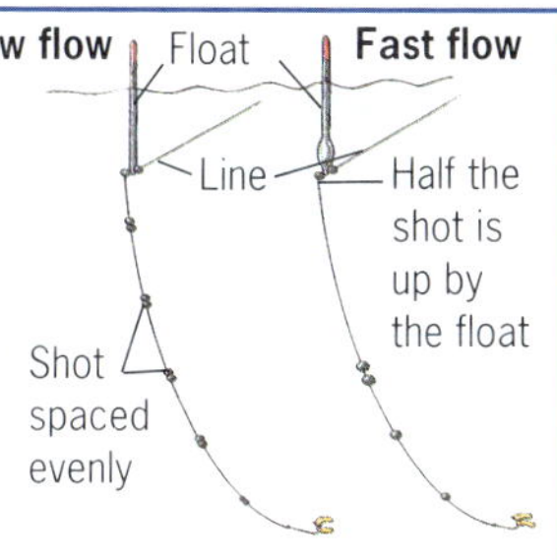

Your guide to the ide

The ide is a bit of a nomad: moving from estuaries to rivers and sometimes lakes. It looks similar to the chub.

FLOAT RIG

With a float set-up like this 'drop rig' (see below) most of the shot is close to the float. The weight of the bait plus some tiny shot means the bait will drop slowly through the water. It's an all-purpose rig that can catch fish at any depth, and the sensitive float will register the smallest bite.

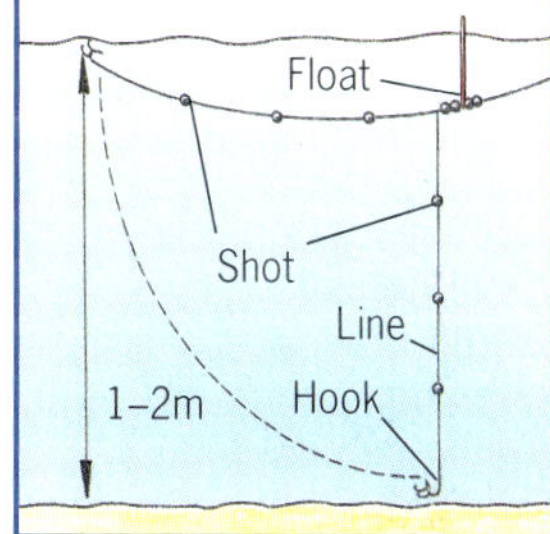

Ways to catch a nase

The nase is often found in deep waters below dams and waterfalls. In major European rivers, such as the Danube and the Rhine, the nase is caught in traps.

ANYONE FOR NASE?

The nase is used as a food in trout farms. In Europe people enjoy smoked, fried and even pickled nase!

The Predators

With its mouthful of sharp teeth, the pike is a born
killer. It preys on fish, frogs and even ducklings.
If you hook a pike – or any of these other predators –
you'll have a fight on your hands.

Deadbait

THE RUNNING LEGER

A pike will happily pick up a deadbait such
as half a mackerel. Once the bait has been
taken, any form of resistance will make the
pike drop it. A running leger tricks the
pike because it allows the line to
be taken without there
being any resistance.
After a short while the
pike will stop to swallow
the bait... that's the time
to wind in your line.

PIKE

LIVEBAIT

Try lip-hooking a small
livebait such as a roach or
rudd onto a size 2 single
hook. This kind of bait can
be used equally well with a
float or leger set-up.

Where and when?
These predators are
pretty widespread.
They are good fish to
catch in winter, because
they will feed when it's
very cold. As with most
fish, the time to try is
at dawn and dusk.

Your bait box
Deadbaits and
worms are your best
bet. Livebaiting is
effective, but it's banned
on some waters.

Mind your fingers
The pike has sharp
teeth, so it's best to
use forceps or pliers to
recover your hook!

The mighty musky

The muskellunge is originally from Canada, and gets its tongue-twisting full name from an Ojibwa Native American word. Like the pike, the musky is a true predator. If food is plentiful it can grow to over 19kg.

THE HUMBLE WORM

Believe it or not, the perfect bait for perch is an ordinary earthworm. In fact there are few fish that will turn their nose up at a big, thick, wriggly worm!

PERCH

ZANDER

A fish called zander

In 1878 a British duke brought a stock of zander from Europe for the lakes on his estate. Today zander are all over the UK. They can be caught with both livebait and deadbait.

Be gentle

Out of the water, zander should be handled with great care and returned to the river as quickly as possible.

Practising on perch

A small perch is likely to be the first fish you will catch. They are very greedy and are sure to go after your maggots. Older perch feed on other fish, including their own young.

PIKING PIRATE

Some anglers are pretty eccentric! There's a Scottish fisherman who raises the 'Jolly Roger' to bring him luck when he's after a really big pike!

From Cats in Combat...

If you fancy fighting a catfish or tracking down an eel... read on!

Catfish

This is a fish with cult status. It's big, ugly and, weight for weight, is the strongest fighter of them all.

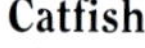

Where and when?

The catfish is widespread in Europe. The best time to catch a catfish is in hot weather, after dark.

Your bait box

Catfish will go for all kinds of baits: mussels, sprats, squid, mackerel, octopus, worms, luncheon meat, liver and even sausages!

Greedy guts!

Like a pike, a catfish will prey on ducklings. They also attack and eat quite big fish: a 24kg cat could take on a 5kg carp.

CATFISH

SUSPENDED DEADBAIT

Try this rig to suspend your deadbait just off the river bed. It will be clearly seen above any rooted weeds and will be more likely to attract a catfish.

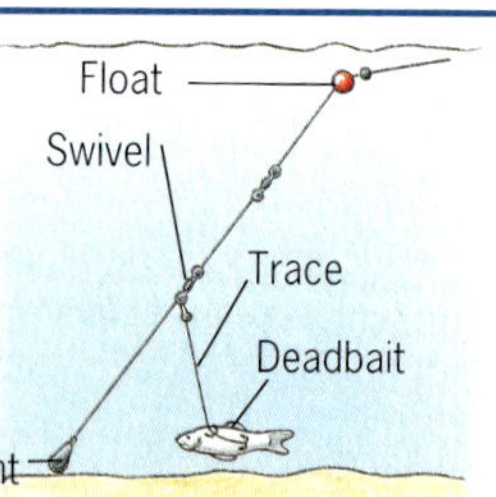

CRAFTY FIGHTERS

Catfish have an unnerving ability to swim backwards as well as forwards which can help them escape the hook. But once landed, they are surprisingly docile and hardly flap a fin!

A DEAD CERT!

Two pieces of squid on a large hook are guaranteed to tempt a catfish. The squid makes a strong-smelling durable deadbait that can be left out in the water for long periods of time. The rig is simple – you need a 60g legerweight stopped by a swivel to which you fix up the deadbait on a length of trace made from a soft but strong braided line.

...to the Elusive Eel

The eel has an odd life cycle. Adult eels spawn in the Sargasso Sea, 7,000km away from parts of Europe and North Africa. The Gulf Stream carries the tiny young across the Atlantic. They take 3 years to reach Europe, where the eels, now adults, enter river systems. After 4 to 12 years, the adults leave their freshwater homes to return to the Sargasso Sea.

Fly Fishing Tackle

Here's the fly fishing tackle you'll need for that perfect casting technique.

Rods

A fly rod is made from carbon fibre which resists bending and gives a good cast. The reel fitting is placed right at the very end of the rod handle which makes the rod well-balanced.

Free reeling

In fly fishing, the reel simply stores the line. To cast a line, you must first pull off enough from the reel for the cast. When a fish is hooked, you pull the line back through your fingers as you hold the rod, trapping it against the cork handle when the fish pulls hard!

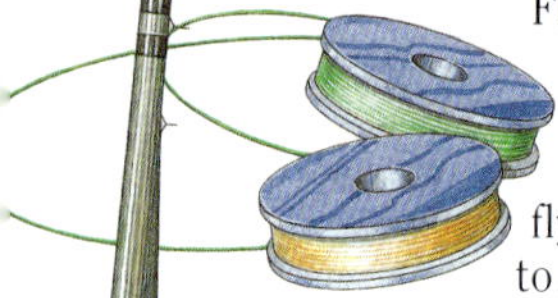

Flying colours

Fly lines come in an amazing range of colours which help you to spot movement of the line which might mean a bite. Some fly lines are made to float, others to sink, and some to do both. Which one you choose all depends on how deep you think the fish will be in the water.

DON'T FORGET

1 Sunglasses not only cut down on surface glare from the water, they also protect your eyes in case your cast 'backfires'.

2 Always carry a 'priest' to kill your catch humanely and quickly.

TAPERING LINES

Fly lines are usually 25m long and they are tapered and weighted. This is because there is no legerweight and to cast a fly you have to rely on the weight of the line itself.

Alluring lures

Lures are large flashy flies that provoke fish into attack. The dog nobbler has a heavy lead head which makes it wiggle through the water. The booby has two buoyant eyes which cause the lure to keep bobbing up to the surface.

FIVE FAB LURES

TYING A FLY

Wind a thread down from the eye to the bend of the hook. Fix some fluorescent green wool at the bend.

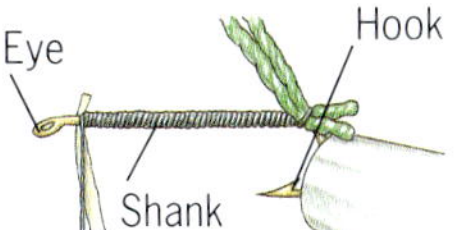

Wind some white wool down the shank to the hook, then back to the eye and fix it.

Bring the green wool over the back of the fly and fix with two turns of thread. Make a tail by 'picking out' the green thread.

You've now tied a baby doll!

FATAL FISHING

The excitement of catching the salmon of his dreams proved too much for one retired colonel. He was found, together with his landed salmon, on the banks of a river... both had expired!

Fair Game

Game fishing for salmon and trout was once the sport of the rich. Today anyone can have a go. Unlike coarse fish, game fish can be taken home for the pot.

THE ART OF CASTING

1 With a good length of line out in front, bring the rod up sharply.

2 Stop the rod in the vertical (12 noon) position – this makes the line shoot out behind you.

3 Once the line is straight out behind you, bring the rod forward quickly.

4 The line will come over your head and shoot out in front.

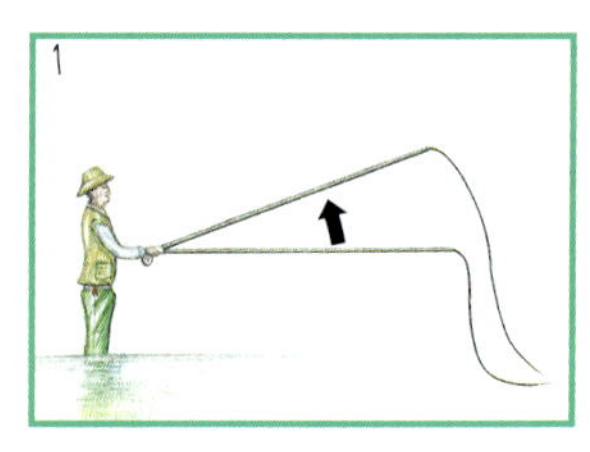

Spawning salmon

Salmon can grow huge: fish up to 24kg have been caught. In winter they swim inland for spawning. They are fat and don't need to feed again until after spawning. However, luckily for the fly fishing angler, they do retain a biting reflex for some weeks! As they swim upstream, salmon can jump up to 3m out of the water to clear rocky rapids.

Spot the difference

Telling a brown trout from a salmon can be tricky. The brown trout does not migrate and older fish often shelter from the river's current behind stones and roots.

Rainbow fish

Rainbow trout have a broad purple band along their side and a black spotted tail fin.

TASTY TREAT

There's nothing a salmon likes better than a juicy, freshwater shrimp. The bite on the bait will almost yank the rod out of your hand!

WET OR DRY?

Choose your fly to suit the fish you're after. Dry flies sit on the water:
1 Walker's red sedge.
2 Grey duster.
Wet flies are cast below the surface:
3 Mallard & claret.
4 Black pennell.

Going for a Spin

Spinning fans go fishing armed with a huge array of artificial lures including plugs, spoons and spinners. Predatory fish such as pike, perch, salmon and trout are provoked into chasing after these lures.

Rod 'n' reel

You need a strong rod for spinning: around 3m long with a screw winch fitting to fix the reel in place. The rod rings are lined with a hard ceramic material to resist wear from constant casting. A fixed spool reel is a must for spinning: and with a heavy spoon you may be able to cast out to a distance of 80m.

Plugs and spoons

Plugs are fish-shaped and made from wood, plastic or metal. Some have a 'vane' attached to the head of the plug which makes it dive in the water when you retrieve the line. Other plugs float and are jointed so that they wriggle. Spoons are the classic spinning lures. They come in many colours and finishes and often they will bring you luck on days when fish won't look at anything else.

THE SPINNING RIG

Predatory fish have a habit of biting through the line, so a short wire trace is useful. This has a swivel at one end tied to the reel line and a 'snap-link' swivel at the other for quick attachment of the plug, spoon or spinner.

HOW TO SPIN

The secret of spinning is to cast out the lure, let it sink, then retrieve it in a series of fast-slow sequences. This is done by alternating the speed with which you wind the reel handle: quickly then slowly. The rod can be moved up and down at the same time which makes the lure move haphazardly in the water. Get ready for action at any moment and don't forget to grip the rod firmly, because when a fish 'strikes' you'll get a violent tug.

Arctic char

The char lives in cold clear lakes in the British Isles, Finland, North America, Greenland and Iceland. It's an excellent game fish to catch on spinner or fly.

American brook trout

A brook trout has large jaws, a mottled back, and white edging to its fins. It feeds on insects, worms and small fish.

GOURMET GUTTING

Follow this step-by-step guide, but ask for an adult's help.

1 Make an incision under the gill cover, and cut downwards towards the chin.

2 Cut along the trout's tummy starting near the anal fin and ending under the chin.

3 Remove all the innards. Wash out thoroughly and remove fins and head if you wish.

4 Trout is delicious baked in foil with herbs and butter. The pink flesh comes away easily from the bones.

BON APPETIT!

25

Harbour Harvests

Fishing from a pier can be fun... you may even catch your supper! You'll be surprised by the number of fish that swim around the rusty iron pillars of a pier.

Your bait box
The first choice for pier fishing is a lugworm. Lugworms burrow in the sand and you can dig them up at low tide. Mussels and peeler crabs also work well.

THE RUNNING LEGER

You'll need a heavy legerweight to hold to the bottom against the tide. The running leger consists of a bead, swivel, legerweight and a 60–180cm length of trace with a strong hook on the end.

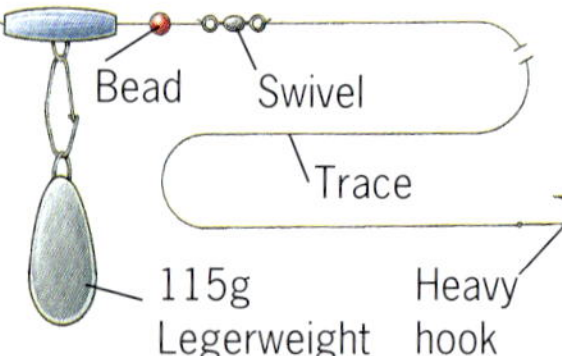

Robust rods and reels

Pier rods are usually 2–3m. They are used with lines of up to 9kg breaking strain. The large heavy reel is held securely by a screw winch fitting.

Get in gear
The multiplier reel has special gearing to let you wind in the line with minimum effort.

PIER PRESSURE!

While fishing off piers and harbour walls, passers-by will keep asking you, "Have you caught anything yet?" When you do eventually catch a fish you'll suddenly become the centre of attention!

Tasty turbot

The turbot belongs to the 'flat fish' family and is unusual in having both eyes on the same side of its head. It lives on the sea bed, eating worms and small mussels. The upper surface of a turbot is covered with bony lumps so it's very rough to the touch.

Flat flounder

The flounder shares the same habitats as its cousin, the turbot. But in winter, it leaves the shore and moves further out to sea. Like turbot, fresh flounder is delicious to eat.

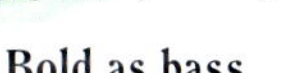

Bold as bass

Bass can be caught from a pier or a boat. They are fierce fighters that will test light tackle to the limit. They love to eat sand eels and peeler crabs.

Mulling over your mullet

Mullet are often seen swimming near the surface in shoals. They may look easy to catch but they are fussy feeders, and it can be hard to find a bait that will tempt them.

Angling Afloat

Fishing on the open sea is exciting. Your skipper may take you out to fish over an old shipwreck, because wrecks act as a magnet for many fish species.

BASIC GEAR

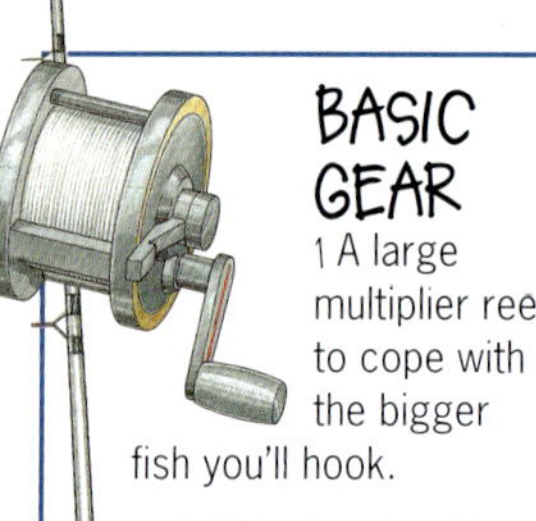

1 A large multiplier reel to cope with the bigger fish you'll hook.

2 A 20kg boat rod is ideal. These rods are 2–2.7m long and are made to stand rough treatment.

4 Super tough monofil line with at least 20kg breaking strain.

5 Heavy legerweights: from 100–200g, depending on the strength of the tide.

Your bait box

Try strips of fish, peeler crabs, sections of mackerel, squid, sand eels and pirks (shiny heavy metal lures which you haul up and down in the water).

Fishing with feathers

'Feathering' for mackerel is the best way to catch these fish. Use about 25m of heavy line. Six short traces, each finished with a hook and some feathers, are fixed onto the line. All you do is lower the line – with a heavy legerweight on the end – over the side of the boat and pull it up and down. It's possible to catch a mackerel on every hook!

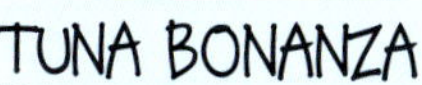

COD

Cod on a rod

UK trawlers net 13,500 tonnes of cod every year, but cod can be caught on rod and line too. Your best bet is to try for cod between October and March. Take care when removing the hook: a cod can swallow your hand with its huge mouth!

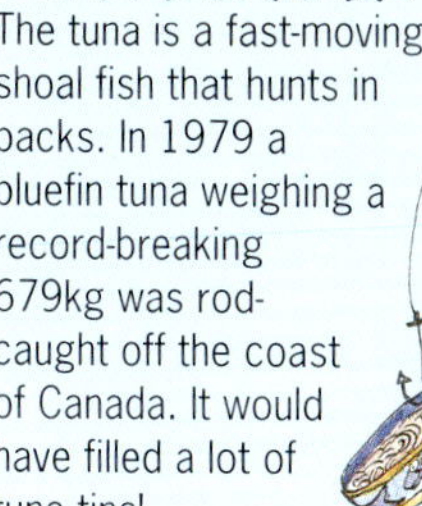

TUNA BONANZA

The tuna is a fast-moving shoal fish that hunts in packs. In 1979 a bluefin tuna weighing a record-breaking 679kg was rod-caught off the coast of Canada. It would have filled a lot of tuna tins!

CONGER EEL

A slippery customer

Conger eels are giant fish that love to live around shipwrecks. 'Wrecking for conger' has many fans: monsters of up to 45kg have been caught. They are strong fighters and, in common with other eel-like fish, can swim backwards.

Powerful pollack

This tasty fish will often hang around with cod. Try using a pirk to tempt one onto your hook.

POLLACK

SAFETY FIRST

Never fish from a boat without wearing a life-jacket. No fish or fishing trip is worth drowning for!

Shark Quest

Sharks are the ultimate challenge. They're big, scary and greedy!

True blue

After films like 'Jaws' we think of all sharks as man-eaters, but this is rarely the case. The blue shark eats fish and has hardly ever been known to attack humans. In the UK the biggest blue shark ever caught was a 99kg monster, hooked in 1959.

Rubby dubby
Sharks can catch a whiff of this evil-smelling bait of minced fish from a great distance.

PUMPING YOUR HOOKED FISH

1 You need to put on a strong harness that lets you stand up and 'fight' a fish.

2 Bring the rod towards you as sharply as you can.

3 Lower the rod, winding the slackened line quickly onto your reel at the same time. Repeat steps 2 and 3 to bring the fish towards your boat.

Hooked!
For sharks you need giant hooks. Besides size, the hook needs to be extra strong. A size 14/0 (shown here life-size) is not too big for a 450kg great white shark.

SURPRISING SIZES
• Great white shark – the biggest of the lot: specimens over 9m have been recorded.
• Blue shark – the biggest can grow to 3m.
• Barracuda – up to 1.5m long, these fish can weigh 14kg.
• Tope – usually under 2m long.

TOPE

Cult status
The tope is the blue shark's smaller cousin. It tends to come nearer the shore. Recently, the tope has gained many fans... it has become an 'in' fish!

Barracuda
With its long slim body, big mouth, and razor sharp teeth, this is the pike of the sea. The barracuda can be caught on lures.

BARRACUDA

INDIGESTION?
Some incredible objects have been found inside sharks: car door handles, dogs, fur coats, metal buckets and plastic washing-up basins, to name a few.

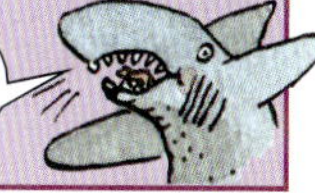

INDEX

Written by Chris Ball
Designed by Brian Robins

First published in 1996 by HarperCollins
Children's Books,
A Division of HarperCollins Publishers
Ltd, 77–85 Fulham Palace Road,
London W6 8JB

ISBN: 0 00 197936 1

Illustrations: Sandra Doyle, Sarah Fuller,
Charlotte Hard, Chris Orr, Halli Verrinder
Photographs: Ardea London Ltd: 2r, 3bl,
3r; Rodney Coldron: cover, 21, 3tl.

A CIP record for this book is available
from the British Library

Printed and bound in Hong Kong